# their journey

## a memoir of my parents

Milton Zweig

This is dedicated to all the families spread around the world that have been affected by the Holocaust and all other forms of Genocide.

ISBN: 1986514412
ISBN-13: 978-1986514415

Published by Milton Zweig
First printed 2018

Original cover art and design by Kristi Butterworth

There are comprehensive and detailed records of the Holocaust and what happened during those dark days. Uncovering what happened to my family, enabling me to fill in most of the blank spaces of my parents' story, was an emotional and tedious endeavor. Without the help of the following it would have been even more difficult.

*New Synagogue Berlin – Centrum Judaicum Foundation*
*Berlin, Germany*

*Kazerne-Dossin Memorial, Museum, and Documentation Center on Holocaust and Human Rights*
*Mechelen, Belgium*

*The National Archives - UK*
*London, UK*

*National Archives – Czech Republic*
*Prague, Czech Republic*

*United States Holocaust Memorial Museum*
*Washington D.C., USA*

*The State Museum Auschwitz-Birkenau in Oświęcim*
*Oświęcim, Poland*

Special thanks to my parents for being patient with me when I bombarded them with questions and to Kristina when I bombarded her with questions on writing.

CR80

I am bound to them, though I cannot look into their eyes or hear their voices.

I honor their history.

I cherish their lives.

I will tell their story.

I will remember them.

-Author unknown

CR80

# Foreword

On Yom HaShoah, Holocaust Memorial Day,
Israelis pause for two full minutes of silence while
air raid sirens wail. Cars will stop, workers stop,
conversations stop – an entire country stands in
silence to remember one for the most horrific
periods of Jewish history. And then, everyone
continues with their activities. Perhaps, they re-
enter their conversations or errands with a dose of
solemnity. But nonetheless, they embrace the idea
of life moving forward.

When I met Arnold and Lanny in 2001, as their new
Rabbi at Temple Solel in Encinitas, California, they
spoke with accents that reminded me of my German
grandparents and they wore the smiles of two
people embracing each other in love and ever
moving forward in life. Little did I know, that only
a few years later would I serve as the Rabbi for Milt
and his family when I moved to Thousand Oaks.
What luck to find a true mentsch!

In this beautiful tribute to his parents, Milt carefully weaves together the words and photos of Arnold and Lanny and his own painstaking research to recreate a history his family will always remember and lessons a world should never forget.

As Jews in Israel, and indeed around the world, stood silently today remembering six million deaths, it was my honor to read the stories Milt lovingly brought to life.

L' Chaim!
Rabbi Ted Riter

Yom HaShoah – Holocaust Memorial Day
27 Nissan 5778
April 12, 2018

*Preface*

As a youngster growing up in suburban Los Angeles I had many opportunities to hear and learn of the Holocaust and how it directly affected my family and the families of millions of others. My earliest memories of my grandmother are of her sitting at her apartment dining room table playing cards with her fellow Jewish-German Holocaust survivors and seeing the prominent yet fading tattooed numbers on the arms of some of her friends. I had no idea what those numbers meant or why they had them but when I would occasionally run my fingers over the wrinkled skin that held those numbers I swear I could feel the anguish that those friends of my Oma had suffered years earlier.

The sun is slowly setting on those that experienced the Holocaust and are still able to tell their stories.

Soon, it will be dark and the only stories will be in archives, books, and the memories of those that took the time to listen and understand.

This is the story of my parents and the parents of my three siblings. It's the story of the Oma and Opa of many grandchildren, great grandchildren, and generations to follow that need to hear the stories and be taught to Never Forget.  It's the story of two people out of millions with similar stories yet it is unique and needs to be told.

This is the story of survival.

*Milton Zweig*

Thousand Oaks, California
March, 2018

# their journey

## a memoir of my parents

# Arnold

My life started sometime in late 1923. The first nine months of my life were very uneventful and I have no recollections whatsoever. Then, on September 23, 1924, I entered the world which over the years I have seen quite a good portion of.

I was born in Berlin, Germany, the same city in which my mother, Erna, and her father were born, and given the name Arnold. My father, Georg, was born in the town of Elbing on October 15, 1890 which at the time belonged to East Prussia and is now part of Poland under the name of Elblag (pronounced *El*-Blong). My mother and father had another son, Gerhard, who was my older brother by about two years.

I can track my mother's side a little more extensively than my father's, mostly because of the exceptional record and memoirs written by my great-grandfather, Henry Cohn, in 1914. He had written his memoirs in Stettin, Prussia, in honor of his 50th wedding anniversary to his wife, Rosa. I had the honor of translating the complete document to English in 1997. One of Henry's grandsons, Fritz Cohn, completed a partial translation and the manuscript was published in the California Historical Quarterly, Vol. XIX, Number 4 in 1940. Today, I can safely guess that the number of direct descendants of Henry Cohn is close to three hundred individuals spread around the world.

Henry and Rosa Cohn had five children: Minna, Emma, Georg, Carl, and Bruno. My grandmother was Minna and she was the oldest of the five, being born in 1866.

Minna eventually married a gentleman named Salomon Korach and they also had five children: Rudi, Sidonie, Walter, Erna, and Gertrud. Sadly, both Sidonie and Walter died at very young ages and Rudi was killed in World War I.

Erna married Georg Zweig and they established a home for both my older brother and myself in Berlin, Germany and thus begins my story.

The year in which I was born was a relatively quiet year. The Great War as it was called then, and which today is referred to as World War I, was over for almost six years. My father, who had served in the German army in the infantry was stationed in

Russia and had come home unscathed. He was a Second Lieutenant having been decorated with the Iron Cross 2nd Class, known as the Eisernes Kreuz 2 Klasse. His last place of service was in the Russian town of Brest-Litovsk (now in modern day Belarus) which coincidentally was the location of the peace treaty signing between the Bolshevik Government of Russia and the Central Powers in 1918, effectively ending Russia's participation in the Great War.

My father's brother, Norbert, was not so lucky. He served in the Western Front and was wounded in Marne, France, not far from Reims. He unfortunately was not able to survive his injuries and died the following day while being cared for in a field hospital in Épernay. The date was October 27, 1918 when he was at the young age of 21, and only two weeks before the War ended.

Norbert was the youngest of my father's three older brothers having been born on May 29, 1897. The two others were Arthur, July 18, 1892 and Felix, July 2, 1898.

Arthur was a brilliant person. He lost his right arm in the war and despite this handicap he managed to become a successful attorney in Berlin. Unfortunately, he succumbed to a massive heart attack in 1931 leaving behind my aunt Theresa

(Resi) and my two young cousins, Claudia and her sister Felicia. I remember my aunt's hair turning from dark black to white overnight when Felicia, a lovely child, died after a very short illness in 1933.

Felix died in Berlin on January 24, 1936 from tuberculosis despite extensive stays in sanitariums in the German Black Forest and in Switzerland. Vaccines were not in widespread use throughout Germany and the rest of Europe until after World War II and tuberculosis was a major problem around the world when I was young.

ය൫

Thanks to the infusion of large amounts of American dollars and the decisive action taken by the German Finance Minister, Hjalmar Schacht, 1924 began to see the stabilization of the German currency. There was an incredible devaluation during the now legendary period of hyper-inflation which spread havoc to the German economy and impoverished most of the German citizenry. At the end of World War I it took about four German marks to purchase one American dollar but by 1923, the amount of German Marks needed to purchase the dollar was approximately 4.2 *trillion.*

History books are full of situations in which economic strife and instability lends rise to political groups and ideologies that turn out to be bad. For Germany, the term "bad" can be construed as a huge understatement.

Germany was a prime setting for political and social change during post-World War I days. These changes developed fairly quickly until a nationalistic and ultra-conservative political group attempted to consolidate power and lay blame to ethnic groups, especially the Jews, for the country's woes. The German Worker's Party was this group and they had been gaining considerable political strength and leadership by a person named Adolf Hitler. He had changed the party's name to the *Nationalsozialistische Deutsche Arbeiterpartei*, or the National Socialist German Worker's Party, NAZI party for short and this was the world I knew when I was a little kid.

By 1924 Adolf Hitler faced trial for the famous Munich Putsch, or Hitlerputsch, in which a coup was attempted to overthrow the government. He was convicted, sentenced, and placed in the now-closed Landsberg Prison where he dictated *Mein Kampf* to Rudolf Hess. Although Hitler was convicted, the huge amount of publicity surrounding this event enabled him to gain incredible support for his agenda and we all know how that eventually turned out. Hitler was released from prison in December, when I was barely three months old.

Things were getting back to normal after the Great War and after the horrible economic instability. Berlin itself was not destroyed as it was after World War II but due to a lack of construction in the previous decade apartment space was at a real premium. Luckily my parents had found an apartment on Köpenicker Straße*, slightly southeast from the middle of the city, but unfortunately this address was not within a fashionable neighborhood or even a desirable area for that matter. It was a rather depressing location amidst industrial enterprises, factories, and smokestacks. Most of the neighborhood buildings were made of red brick but soot and pollution from all the nearby industry made those same buildings appear almost gray and lifeless. The Reichstag Building which was the seat of German government was maybe an hour walk east while the old historic Brandenburg Gate was only a 45 minute walk away. The ornate and historically significant bridge, the Oberbaumbrücke, was to our east by way of a short five minute walk.

------------
*The German language letter, β, is called an Eszett and is pronounced with a combination of both S and Z.

Behind the apartment building was the Spree River which bisected Berlin and slowly coursed its way westward before meeting up with the Havel River at the old Spandau Citadel. The building we lived in was typical of a style prevalent in proletarian neighborhoods called a *Mietskaserne*, or literally translated, a barracks for renters; a tenement. Our building had three big courtyards with five story high structures on each side of the square. These squares were connected to each other by a passageway and they were situated in-line one after the other with building wings on either side. It is here that I have my very first memories.

It was most likely 1929 and I was four and a half years old. At that age we always mentioned the "half" and I was no exception in proclaiming that whenever the opportunity arose. My first playmate was English speaking; I believe he was American but could very well have been English, perhaps with the name of Randy or Andy. One or two of his little legs were ensconced in some sort of contraption of light brown leather with vertical metal ribs. In retrospect I would surmise that he had some sort of defect causing him to walk awkwardly and that the contraption aided him to develop his legs properly. This left a big impression on me.

I remember spending a lot of time at the very rear of the last building which was fronting the Spree.

With the rebuilding and construction of the German infrastructure and new buildings rapidly being constructed you can imagine the enjoyment a little boy would have by sitting at the river's edge and watching barges laden with coal and all kinds of supplies. I liked to watch the river traffic and try to figure out what everything was and where they were headed. I would watch in awe as deckhands would wedge long poles into the riverbed and hold the upper end against their shoulder while walking from one end of the barge along narrow paths to the other end, all the while propelling the boat in a smooth manner. The barges were very deep in the water and I noticed how the deckhands did their work effortlessly along very narrow walkways only a few inches above the water.

I also remember spending time with my English speaking friend at the river embankment. We were only there a short time before our skin and clothes would become filthy as the air around us was saturated with soot from the industrial smokestacks in the neighborhood. We enjoyed ourselves immensely, looking across the water and shouting while imagining the return echo was that of someone else calling back to us even though we could not see anyone on the other side.

C3ᴇꙨ

The Jewish communities of Germany were organized in a slightly different manner than we know today. There were no private synagogues that would hire a rabbi and there were no non-profit synagogues. Instead, the Jewish community was supported as an entity. Households declared their religious affiliation on supplied government forms and were required to pay a fifteen percent surcharge based on their income tax. This requirement was not just for the Jewish population, but for members of every religion. The government took the collected funds and allocated them to the various religious organizations within Berlin, including the main Berlin Jewish Community association who in turn supported the 15-20 synagogues within the city.

Our household was not a kosher or very religious household but we paid into this system as did most everyone we knew. Although we had the Sabbath candlesticks on display, I don't recall ever seeing my mother light the candles. We attended services at the synagogue infrequently, but went regularly on the major Jewish holidays. My father would fast during the Yom Kippur holiday and my brother and I would try to do the same as we got a little older.

In 1930, my parents moved a little northward into the Berlin suburb of Prenzlauer Berg which was a somewhat nicer neighborhood and we occupied a more modern apartment on Wehlauer Straβe. Probably the best thing I remember about this neighborhood was that we were able to play outside without having our clothes and skin covered in dirt because of pollution.

My father was able to secure our apartment by lending the landlord some money for a second mortgage.  We were considered upper middle class and enjoyed a comfortable apartment with nice furniture and were even able to take occasional family vacations.  I still have fond recollections of the four of us taking a nice summer trip south to the Black Forest and Garmisch-Partenkirchen, the beautiful Bavarian mountain resort.  I think it was the last time our family took such a vacation in Germany.  It was 1932.

CB&O

My brother and I had shared a bedroom.  The winters were usually extremely cold and our  room had a relatively modern freestanding room heater covered in ceramic tiles. We heated the room by feeding it unbelievably large quantities of hard pressed, oblong shaped briquettes of coal.  Each tenant in the building had a small stall in the basement to store their winter supply of coal. I remember there was no light down there and we had to use a kerosene lamp to see our way.

We had a very large and ornate wood armoire in our room where we stored clothes and bedding. It was the main piece of furniture in our room, situated fairly close to the furnace. We placed our beds near the furnace and armoire for warmth. I would often pull myself up to the top of the armoire and jump back down to the bed below. My father enjoyed watching my athletic prowess and I used every opportunity I could to show off. My brother, who had a heart condition, was not able to follow suit and I always believed he was a little envious of that. One night when I was about six years old, my brother and I heard a very large cracking noise while we were trying to sleep. The noise was followed by silence and then another eerie sounding noise a few minutes later. I perked my ears and held my breath not knowing what the noise was. My brother must have done the same and when the noise came back a third time he whispered, "Did you hear this?!"

I whispered back, "Yes!"

By the time we heard the fourth cracking sound we were both utterly scared. My brother jumped out of bed, ran to the window to which all the other apartments faced, opened it, and yelled as loud as possible, "HELP!!" We were alone that night as my parents went to the theater or something. Our neighbors, hearing the yell from my brother, came rushing to help us thinking there were burglars or something of the like within our apartment. They searched under the beds and in the armoire but found nothing. It wasn't until the next morning when we realized the cause of the horrible cracking noise. The heat in the room had caused the side of the wooden armoire to split! Such were the dangers of apartment heating in the late 1920s!

In the beginning of 1930 I was sent to a nursery school of about fifteen children. The lady who took care of us was Tante (Aunt) Minnich. I remember her name to this day but curiously enough, whenever my mother had asked me over the years about that time in nursery school, I denied remembering any of it, and even after repeated prodding I pretended I could not remember the name of the lady. I do recall doing some fun handicrafts while at the nursery school. We were taught to do creative weaving by threading narrow strips of colored, fabric-like paper into horizontal and vertical patterns while varying the spaces between each "thread". The results were nice colorful patterns and the art activities never bored me.

One day I came home from nursery school and told my mother that we were having a costume party and that I would like to dress as a clown. My mother was very handy when it came to sewing and she fabricated a marvelous costume for me. My outfit consisted of a tall pointy cone shaped hat with a matching blouse and baggy pants made of white cloth imprinted with large green polka dots. Around my collar I wore a white ruffled and frilly piece of fabric. The day of the party arrived and my mother took me, excited to see all the other mother-made costumes. Much to her surprise, nobody had a costume on except for me. The whole costume party was just an invention of mine.

I was bored and starting to get a little restless as I really wanted to start school prior to my next birthday. Back then, the German school year started after Easter and luckily for me the registration deadline in 1930 was having a birth date prior to October 1924. I had made the deadline by only two weeks and was able to attend a public school that was only a five minute walk from our apartment. Nevertheless, regardless of the proximity of the school, in the four years I attended that school I was late very often.

My first-grade teacher was a gentleman named Mr. Lemke. What he taught and how he taught it I really don't know. What I do remember is that for

whatever infractions committed by the students he
would grab us by the little hairs of our sideburns
and pull us up until we stood on our tippy toes…
and then he would pull just a little bit more.  I
suppose back then if we complained about that sort
of treatment our parents would just tell us to behave
better the next school day.

Of all the four years at that school I pretty much
remember nothing about the things that were taught
to me except that the Depression had taken hold in
Germany and warm milk was dispensed to poor
children in the school basement while others were
given certificates for haircuts at a local barber.  At
one time the teacher asked all the students of our
all-boys class, as to the occupations of our fathers.
Mostly they were blue collar type of jobs with a few
firemen, policemen, and business people such as my
own father who worked as a cost estimator and
buyer for a garment manufacturer.  One of the local
factories, a gas factory that converted coal to
cooking gas, decided to tear down their large
chimney.  Because one of the student's fathers was
a fireman, we were all invited to witness the
demolition.  We carefully watched them drill holes
in strategic spots around the chimney, place
explosives within the holes, and detonate the thing.
The chimney leaned sideways a bit, broke in two or
three pieces, and came crashing down.  The

spectacle beat school anytime!!  This I remember....
school I do not.

CHBO

In January 1933 Hitler came to power and shortly
thereafter we started having air raid drills even
though it would be another six years before the war
began.  Teachers who had previously worn swastika
pins on the underside of their lapel, flashing them to
only trusted friends, now sported them on the front
side for everyone to see.  Students started attending
school wearing the uniforms of the Hitler Youth and
practiced the official greeting of *Heil Hitler!* along
with the proper angle to raise their arm in salute.  Of
course, as an eight year old, it was unfathomable to
know what ramifications and historical discourse
these actions would cause.

Some sort of quasi-military discipline was also
initiated.  A student leader positioned himself
outside the classroom and at the sight of the
approaching teacher would shout *ACHTUNG!*
whereupon all the students got to their feet, stood
ramrod straight, and as the teacher entered the room
would shout in unison *Heil Hitler!*  I stayed in that
school and progressed normally for four years

leaving at Easter in 1934.

The German school system at that time had several possibilities for advancement. A student could stay in the type of public school like I was in for a full eight years and upon completion have successfully achieved a basic education. This would allow them to start working as an apprentice in any of the trades such as a baker, carpenter, printer, or get business training. Those apprenticeships, which usually paid the employee a pittance, lasted usually four and sometimes five years. At the end of the apprenticeship period, often coupled with a trade school for theoretical instruction, the apprentice would hopefully pass some field specific exams and become a Journeyman. After another couple of years and an additional exam, the Journeyman would become a Master and receive his Master's Certificate. Only one with a Master's Certificate could hire and train apprentices but only in a limited number. This was to avoid having unscrupulous Masters hiring only apprentices as they were considered cheap labor.

A second option for a student was to transfer to a Gymnasium (High School) after their first four years of public school. The Gymnasium had an eight-year curriculum including subjects such as chemistry, physics, humanities, Greek and Latin, math, and more and were intended to be preparatory for those students who would eventually be qualified to attend a university. Admission to a university required graduation from a Gymnasium along with good grades.

The third option for students wishing to have a better education which would allow them to enter a wider spectrum of jobs other than those reserved for university graduates, was to enter a school offering a six-year curriculum. These schools, called *Mittel Schule*, or Middle School, were not as narrowly geared to the needs of blue collar workers but more to the needs of business people, administrators, supervisors, etc. Upon completion of Middle School, graduates typically did not attend a university, instead began an apprenticeship with increased chances of advancement.

In the spring of 1934 my parents moved again. This time we moved to a more comfortable apartment on Manfred-von-Richthofen Straße in the south-central Berlin district of Templehof-Schöneberg, near the site of Berlin's Templehof Airport. Although we lived a couple blocks away from the western edge of the airport, we were not at all inconvenienced by the sound of the loud propeller planes (there were no commercial jet aircraft yet) as the airport was still under construction.

In the four years that we lived in that neighborhood

Templehof Airport was a major hub of construction activity. The old airport was destined to become a major transportation hub to aid the Nazis for their upcoming war effort. Hitler himself visited the airport during the construction process and wanted it to be a showcase to the world. Much to his delight the construction effort succeeded and the airport became one of the busiest airports in Europe and boasted one of the largest terminals in the world at the time. All this was of course after we fled Germany in 1938.

The airport held renewed importance after World War II when it became the hub for the Berlin Airlift of 1948-1949. This immense and well documented humanitarian mission was necessary when the Soviets blocked all transport of vital supplies into West Berlin, isolating 2.5 million citizens. The Soviets did leave a little airspace into the airport and the U.S. and British military took advantage of it by flying in tons and tons of much needed food and supplies to the citizens.

Templehof Airport eventually ceased operations in 2008 and became a public park and recreation area. Today, the remaining buildings and land are in the planning stages for cultural districts, museums highlighting the Allied presence, and a visitor center.

Our neighborhood in 1934 was good but the political situation was getting worse. Adolf Hitler and the Nazi Party were gaining political momentum at a dizzying pace. I was only nine years old and did not know all the political comings and goings but I did see that the Jewish people were being targeted more and more. Hitler became the official Führer and Chancellor in the summer and his followers were already at work spreading the hatred that he craved. Regulations and rules that prohibited Jews from owning land, holding certain professional degrees, being newspaper editors, and much more had already been in effect since 1933 but now there were more instances of Jews being singled out with anti-Semitic actions. As far as I recall, my parents didn't talk about this situation all too much. In retrospect, I am sure they spoke about the situation the Jews and our family were facing well out of earshot of both my brother and I so that we wouldn't be scared or worried. I'll never know the conversations they had but I do know that my parents decided I would be attending a Jewish school because of the ever increasing anti-Semitism present in the regular schools.

There were about 1,300 students enrolled at the magnificent Oranienburger Straße Synagogue but because of the sudden influx of all the Jewish kids I was assigned to an annex building next to the giant synagogue. The lowest level of classes, like the one I was in, was very crowded and we were separated into three classes of about fifty-five students each. Adjacent to the rear of this annex was a Jewish cemetery that held the graves of many, including the 17th Century Jewish philosopher, Moses Mendelssohn. Our recess times were spent playing amongst the graves while winter snowball battles were held with the tall headstones acting as wonderful parapets. The outer cemetery pathway was our track for running races and other events.

The Oranienburger Straße synagogue was built in the Moorish Revival style and opened in 1866. It was a large facility, seating thousands of people and had the distinction of being the largest synagogue in all of Germany. The building had a great existence before the Nazis took over, even hosting a violin concert by Albert Einstein. The building and its surrounding neighborhood saw dark days starting around 1938 when Kristallnacht occurred and the Nazis looted, desecrated the synagogue, and tried to burn it down. A local police officer on duty, a non-Jew, saved the building by brandishing a gun and telling the Nazis to get lost. Unfortunately, the Battle of Berlin in 1943-1944 saw heavy damage caused by the Allied bombing and in the late 1950s the remainder of the structures were demolished. It wasn't until the Berlin Wall came down in 1989 that a serious reconstruction project took place and the magnificent structure came back to life and reopened in 1995. Today, the gilded dome is visible for miles and the neighborhood is a pleasant area of outdoor cafes and well-kept apartments.

At the time of my enrollment in this beautiful setting, I was given a choice of which foreign language I wanted to study. It was either English, followed by French two years later, or the other way around. I chose French first. The Principal was named Dr. Stern and I found out in later years that he actually lived to be 98 years old. I had different teachers for all the various subjects and I remember them all....but not with a great deal of affection.

Herr Loewy was our music teacher. His nickname was "Stift" which literally means pencil or crayon but in slang could mean apprentice or bellboy. I have no idea how he got the nickname but was told by students before me that he had always been called that. For many years after those school years old classmates still referred to him as "Stift". When we were required to sing in class, I was mostly excused from the exercise because I could not carry a tune. I could never comprehend the nuances of reading music and musical notes and frankly really didn't care as I just hated it all together.

My Hebrew teacher's name was Herr Smolinsky.

He was had a crippled leg which he always dragged behind him. He had a heavy walking stick which was used more often as a weapon to hit us than to walk with. Needless to say, I hated that class also. German and French was taught by Herr Dr. Rosenberg who was a cool professional and I found him acceptable as an instructor. Math and physics were taught by Herr Simson, who was a demanding teacher but in a manner that garnered respect from the students and inspired them as well. Art class was taught by Herr Geismar who also had a nickname lasting for generations. He was called "Greis" which is slang for Old Man.

When I was eleven years old, Berlin hosted the Olympic Games. The games were awarded to the city in 1931 and at the time the government intended to just renovate the old Olympic Stadium which was originally slated to be used in the 1916 Olympic Games. However, because of the outbreak of World War I the 1916 games never took place. With the Nazi party taking power in 1933 Hitler saw the opportunity to showcase Germany using the Olympics as a backdrop and he built the new and grandiose Olympiastadion which held about 100,000 people. They used the Olympic Games purely as a propaganda tool. All eyes would be on our country and Hitler had his opportunity to show the world how his vision of a unified, peaceful, and tolerant Germany. In the weeks leading up to the Games the Nazis attempted to gloss over the atrocities towards certain groups, especially the Jewish people of Berlin. I remember seeing bus benches with the words *Nicht für Juden*, Not for Jews, painted over so that the growing antisemitism would be hidden from the world. Acts like this were common and the city actually had a festive feel to it for a short time. Odd side note, this was also the first time I had ever seen a black man.

Many people feel the Olympic Games turned out to be a black eye for the Nazis but that's not actually true. Before the games had begun there was a concerted effort by the international community to boycott the Olympics under the guise of human rights violations. Much of the basis of these protests came out of the Nazi decree named the Nuremberg Race Laws of 1935 which basically stated that Jews were no longer German citizens. When these boycott efforts failed it pretty much legitimized the Nazi run Olympic Games and the Hitler regime. Many people feel that the black American, Jesse Owens, who won more medals than anyone else, eroded that Aryan sentiment but that really wasn't true as the Germans won more medals than any other country during those games.

My schooling and Jewish education eventually led me to being a Bar Mitzvah, the age at which a

Jewish boy becomes morally responsible for his actions and is considered a full-fledged member of the Jewish community. My Bar Mitzvah Shabbat service and ceremony was held at the old Oranienburger Straße synagogue. Unfortunately, this would be the last time for many years that I stepped foot in a synagogue.

By 1938 antisemitism and Jewish restriction in everyday life was reaching the tipping point. It became intolerable for a Jewish person to live in Berlin or anywhere in Germany. Although the war had not yet broken out, many Jewish citizens had packed up and left for safer havens. My grandmother's brothers were leaving the country for Palestine (Israel) and my friends and their families were leaving, resulting in classrooms that suddenly had numerous empty seats, a vast difference than when I first enrolled in an overcrowded school four years earlier. In retrospect, 1938 marked the very last time that I would be in a classroom or any school setting. I was only thirteen years old.

Many laws were instituted and designed to deprave the Jews of their dignity and of their existence. Identification cards were required to have the name "Sarah" or "Israel" added as a middle name and a large red "J" was imprinted on passports.

Getting a visa to leave was really not the problem.

In fact, history shows that the non-Jews and Nazis reacted with pleasure to seeing waves of Jews leaving their beloved Germany. To get a visa one merely needed to go to the local police station and inform them that they planned to leave and their passport would be stamped with an exit visa.

The problem? Getting a visa to *enter* a country, any country, at this time was extremely difficult and getting more problematic to do with every passing day.

Conversations among the adults consisted of basically one topic, leaving Germany, and would sound something like this:

"Are you leaving?"

"Where are you going?"

"How are you getting there?"

"What's required to get there?"

When other countries got tired of the large influx of émigrés they closed their borders, effectively trapping millions of Jewish people in Europe.

My father had reacquainted himself with a business associate named Erich Scheidemann in the summer of 1938. They had made an arrangement in which Erich would receive calls on our phone for the sole purpose of obtaining visas for both his and our families. One day we received a phone call from an unidentified lady. She had left a message for Mr. Scheidemann to call her as soon as possible. When he didn't call, she had left a second message and finally a third message. My father was perturbed and asked him 'Why do you not call this lady back? At least give her the courtesy of a phone call." Erich insisted that she was only calling because she wanted help in getting her son a visa. He called her back finally and learned that actually her son had already been able to obtain a visa, while in Frankfurt, to enter the country of Colombia.

The very next day my mother and Mr. Scheidemann made their way to Frankfurt to this newly found source of visas to obtain the same for our respective families.

They arrived at the private residence of some sort of honorary consulate member who had connections to Colombia. In a short time, he whipped out some blank paper, placed it in his old typewriter, and generated visas for seven people eager to emigrate from Germany to Colombia.

Shortly after returning to Berlin they received a phone call explaining that our visas were missing some important stamps and they had to return to Frankfurt to have them applied. It was a minor delay and gave my brother and myself some time to pull our old world atlas off the dusty shelf to actually see where in the world this country called Colombia was!

During the search for visas my parents had decided to downsize our living quarters. We moved again, this time to a smaller apartment in the middle of Berlin, on Seydel Straβe, and they systematically sold much of our furniture and non-essential belongings to make a quicker departure once it was possible.

Sure enough, once we had our papers in order it took only four weeks to complete our final preparations, say goodbye to our remaining friends and family, and vacate our apartment. We were on a train out of Berlin on September 24, 1938, my fourteenth birthday and only six weeks before Kristallnacht.

From left, Georg Zweig, Norbert Zweig,
Arthur Zweig
Elbing, East Prussia, 1906

Felix Zweig
Germany, 1933

Georg (R) sitting with his fellow soldiers at the end of WWI.
Russia, 1917

Arrow points to Arthur. This is the front of a postcard
sent in early 1918 to Georg. Arthur's note on the back
explains that he has lost an arm in the war.

Georg (R) with a fellow German soldier
Date and location unknown

Arnold Henry Zweig
About 1926
Berlin, Germany

their journey

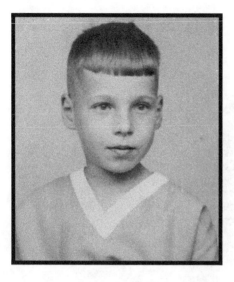

Arnold
1931
Berlin, Germany

Arnold (R) with Gerhard
1929
Berlin, Germany

Arnold
1934
Berlin, Germany

Arnold
Berlin, Germany 1930

Arnold, left, with his parents and brother.
Garmisch-Partenkirchen
1932
Berlin, Germany

Arnold, bottom right on the grass, with his class.
About 1935
Berlin, Germany

My family and the Scheidemann family, seven of us, made our way to the port of LeHavre, France, via Paris. We boarded a magnificent ship called the SS Colombie. It was probably the largest ship I had seen and certainly much larger than any of the barges I had seen along the Spree when I was little. The large white ship with the two smokestacks painted bright red were our ride to a new life and our escape from the oppressive hatred and antisemitism that began to take over Germany. I couldn't wait to board although was I sad that my grandmother Minna had decided to stay in Germany, a decision that would come back to haunt all of us.

The 22-day trip to Colombia was fairly uneventful although there was one funny thing that happened. We were on board during Rosh Hashanah and we had informed the crew of the Jewish New Year holiday. Wanting to please us and make our trip comfortable, they placed hats and noisemakers on the long dining room tables thinking that the holiday was one of merriment and celebration. We had a good laugh about that one. The SS Colombie had stops in exotic ports like Martinique, Curacao, and the large port of La Guaira, Venezuela eventually arriving to the city of Barranquilla, Colombia in a driving tropical rainstorm.

We had absolutely no idea where we would go but, with the aid of a local Jewish assistance group, we were given the equivalent of $20 to take a one hour train ride to the city and find lodging. After travelling in pitch blackness, we found ourselves in town and were able to successfully find a room in the Palace Hotel in where we stayed for about a week prior to renting a proper apartment. My brother and I explored our immediate neighborhood and tried our best to learn Spanish, which for a 14-year-old really doesn't take all too long. Colombia was a completely different world than Berlin. A different culture with dark skinned people speaking Spanish, much warmer and very humid compared to northern Germany, but everyone was extremely nice to us and we did not experience any of the hatred that Germany was embroiled in. In short, we quickly learned to enjoy the community and felt very comfortable there.

Our apartment was shared with the Scheidemann family, as well as one other family, making the place somewhat cramped but we adapted well. My father and Erich Scheidemann were anxious to earn some money and in a short time were able to acquire a quantity of wood from someone's old shipping containers. Now, my father was not a very handy person but Erich was. Together, they created some basic apartment furniture with the wood and after visitors saw their handiwork, began to make furniture for sale to others. This led to them opening a small carpentry shop and they were able to sell their fabrications.

Unfortunately, Erich Scheidemann began to have issues with alcohol and my father decided to end their business relationship.

I was restless to start working as well. Most kids my age in Barranquilla had some sort of work experience and I was eager to fit in with them. My first job I had was very short in tenure. It was at a grocery store called the "Zic Zac" and I had the important job of sweeping the floors, making deliveries, and best of all, roasting the freshly picked Colombian coffee beans. Although I was a pretty good employee, I was eventually terminated from this job because of some mishandling of a large shipment of eggs. Basically, I was riding on the back of my boss' motorcycle over the rough Barranquilla roads and instead of hanging on dearly to the eggs I hung on dearly for my life and in the process, all the eggs fell and broke.

Eventually, my father was able to help me get another job but it took a few months for that to pan out.

After the break with his partner, our apartment had some extra space to rent. Two young gentlemen from an agricultural area of Germany wanted to rent the room to live in and eventually make a product that really wasn't that sought after in Colombia, butter.

They were ready to rent our room and move in immediately if we had a refrigerator to store their butter. So my father went to a store that sold appliances and spoke with the owner, who himself was originally from Austria and spoke German.

"We need a refrigerator but we don't have any money," my father explained.

"What kind of work do you do?" the Austrian answered.

"I am a carpenter."

"Oh! A carpenter! We are moving the store in a short time and will need lots of shelves to be constructed. Here's a refrigerator. Just give me a small down payment and then you can work off the balance when we move by fabricating our new shelves."

Knowing a good business proposition, my father brought the refrigerator home and rented the apartment room to the butter makers. By the way, the butter they made turned out to be the best in town!

Two months later my father fulfilled his obligation by building the extensive display shelves in the new appliance store. While working on the shelves, he asked the owner about the possibility of hiring me for work. Soon, I interviewed for a job in the shop and was hired.

I was employed at that shop, The Todo Electrico, for almost eleven years. Starting at the bottom by cleaning and sweeping floors I had a strong work ethic and worked my way to pretty much running the shop in its entirety. We were, for the most part, an electrical shop and we sold, rented, and leased equipment and supplies. Our biggest clients were contractors but we would sell items in any quantity if need be.

During a large portion of my tenure at Todo Electrico most of Europe, including my hometown of Berlin, was embroiled in War. World War II broke out about eleven months after we fled, with the German invasion of Poland. It lasted until 1945 and it really wasn't until then that people realized the horrors that took place. Over the years, I have been asked "What did people think about the War?", "Did other Jewish refugees say anything?", or "Did you ever know what was happening in Germany?"

Jews began emigrating from Germany to Colombia

starting in 1933. Though the totals listed in historical literature vary, one could safely estimate that there were approximately 5,000 Jews that came to Colombia. In fact, the Colombian police ran a census in 1939, counting a total of 3,474 German Jewish refugees but that figure seems wholly incomplete. Most of the Jews were living in the capital city of Bogotá with a considerably smaller number in my town of Barranquilla.

There was not much conversation from newer refugees about the horrors of the war. Many, if not all, had left behind family and friends. We eventually learned that my maternal grandmother, Minna, who decided to stay in Germany when we left for Colombia, was taken to the Theresienstadt Ghetto in the summer of 1942 and she died after only six months. There was nothing we could do to help her and the others. We were consumed with working and trying to forget the past; we all wanted to just move on with our lives.

Minna Korach was one day shy of her 77th birthday when she was taken by the Nazis out of Berlin on July 27, 1942. She had lived alone in an apartment in the middle of the city just on the outskirts of the large Tiergarten Park. She was elderly and most likely having a hard time getting around and filling her meager food rations. Perhaps she had neighbors that watched over her or an old friend that would share crusty bread or some soup. We'll never know all the details surrounding her last free days.

What we do know is that the elderly people were useless to the Nazis. Elderly Jewish Germans like my grandmother were not strong enough to staff the slave labor positions that so many German companies instituted. The factories and shops that fueled the German war effort were well known in this regard and ultimately paid large amounts of money in war reparations to survivors and their families. Those in forced labor were severely mistreated and abused. Many died at the hands of their so-called employers. It is estimated that close to ten million Europeans, including 1.3 million concentration camp inmates, were ultimately subjected to this horrible existence. German companies such as Daimler-Benz, Philips, Volkswagen, Krupp, and Siemens are only a few of many German companies that were guilty of such war horrors.

Many of the concentration camps operated by the Nazis had large wrought iron signs outside the entrance gates that read *Arbeit Macht Frei*, Work Brings Freedom, which attempted to appease the fears of incoming prisoners. They wanted prisoners to have the impression that hard work and obedience in these camps would earn the ultimate result of their release which of course was a complete and horrible fabrication. My grandmother was taken to a camp like this when the Nazis deported her on the *Alterstransport #1/31*, the Old People's Transport, with ninety-nine other people.

Theresienstadt Ghetto was located in the German controlled country of Czechoslovakia in an old town called Terezín. History shows that the Holy Roman Emperor from 1765 to 1790, Joseph II, ordered the construction of a fort to prevent Prussian troops from invading land under his control. The fort was named Theresienstadt in honor of his mother, Maria Theresa. One bit of irony about Joseph II is that he abolished both the death penalty and serfdom during his reign, a complete contrast to what his Theresienstadt became years later. Another note about Joseph II; he was the brother of Marie Antoinette and, although estranged from his sister, he tried in vain to hatch an escape plan for her to leave France during the French Revolution.

The camp had a slightly different administrative setup than most of the other concentration camps and this led to the appearance that the camp was just a ghetto and not like other facilities around Europe. For example, those that were incarcerated were under the control of the Jewish Council of Elders who reported to the German authorities. Those in charge of the camp, the *Schutzstaffel*, commonly referred to as the SS, really didn't care what the Jewish people were doing within Theresienstadt unless it was some sort of rebellious or breaking of the rules issue. For the most part, this Jewish Council of Elders helped inmates with all sorts of activities within the camp and could have been seen as a sort of City Council for a small community.

When Minna arrived at the camp she was one of 32,878 Jewish residents of Germany that were deported in 1942. Of those, the first deportees from Berlin only started arriving to Theresienstadt one month earlier than Minna. She was not tattooed but assigned a number nonetheless, 2387. Most likely upon arrival she was met by someone from the Jewish Council, or perhaps someone from the SS, and then assigned into the barracks of elderly Jewish women. The elderly barracks have been described as being like dark dungeons with only a single light bulb and little to no heating. They were on the third floor of the barracks, much like an attic. The floors were not smooth concrete but irregular with broken flooring material jutting out just waiting for an elderly lady to wander by in the dark. The quarters had rafters open to the exterior, allowing the hot sun and ice-cold winter to enter. The situation in the camp had been dire before Minna's arrival with children and adults dying on a daily basis, often with fifty elderly dying in a day.

By August of 1942 the camp became extremely overcrowded with the stench of dead and sick people often filling the cramped rooms. The dead were left in their rooms and barracks for a full day in the heat until they were carried out. Food often consisted of moldy bread or thin grey lentil soup. Thousands were transported out of the camp to their death at places like Auschwitz or Bergen-Belsen just to make room for additional transports to drop off their human cargo. The Jewish Council tried their best to facilitate some sort of harmony within the camp and to prevent an increasing number of Jews being sent out to certain death but to no avail.

By the beginning of 1943, when Minna was there for only six months, the notorious Adolf Eichmann found the Theresienstadt Ghetto to be too crowded and decided to send increasing numbers of prisoner transports directly to Auschwitz and to a sure death. Included in this edict was the inclusion of young children that had previously been immune to deportation transports. These transports commenced on January 20, 1943 and four days later Minna died. She died not in a gas chamber or by some bizarre Nazi medical experiment but supposedly by heart failure, most likely exacerbated by the extreme winter cold and perhaps at seeing little children being sent to their death. Although her death certificate states heart failure it's entirely possible that she died of starvation or any other illness as well.  She died not with her family by her side but with other Jews that were forced to endure this genuine pit of humanity alongside her.

※

The Jews in Colombia that survived the Holocaust just wanted to move forward with their lives. I was the same.  I worked tirelessly at Todo Electrico and tried to assimilate into the Colombian fabric and get on with my life.  Other refugees arrived in Barranquilla after my family did and we tried to help them much as others had helped us.  We didn't dwell on their experiences in the Old Country except to find out which community they came from and such.  It wasn't until the concentration camps were fully liberated, and for many years later, which we learned in excruciating detail what happened to those that survived and those who were in hiding for the duration of the war.

※

My parents were friends with another Jewish refugee family from Berlin, Käthe Cohn and her husband Werner. They were living in the Colombian city of Cali, the city to which I had moved to after leaving Todo Electrico to work as a manufacturer's representative. Käthe's niece at the time was living in Bogotá with her mother and had accompanied her Aunt Käthe to Cali for a visit to my parents. At the time, I had a girlfriend and really wasn't looking for another one but as soon as they arrived and walked into my parents' home and I saw Uschi I knew she was the one.

Ursula "Uschi" Lehmann had arrived from Bogotá to Cali with her family on Christmas Eve 1954 and by New Year's Day 1955, one week later, we were engaged to be married. For that one week we spent every waking hour together and were inseparable with sightseeing, dancing, and talking. I was so smitten that I didn't go back to work for almost three weeks, when Uschi had to return to her job in Bogotá and her mother. I had enough money saved up so the break in working really didn't cause any issues for me.

She was twenty-four at the time, Jewish, beautiful, smart, a great dancer, and fun to be with. She had spent most of the war hiding in Belgium after emigrating from Berlin. In fact, for a few short years we lived only a few kilometers from each other in Berlin without knowing each other. We had both suffered losses at the hands of the Nazis and both had stories to tell of our survival and of Germany in general.

In the Yiddish language, there is a word. That word, *Beshert*, is often used to describe a fortuitous pairing, a good match, or the finding of one's soulmate. When one has such a match there is often a feeling that the hand of God had some part in the circumstances that led to two people finding each other. It was comforting to know that after the horrors that both us endured that there was still a God around to create our *Beshert*.

ᘓᘔ

Arnold, seated left, at work in the Todo Electrico store. Arnold was barely
16 years old when this photo was taken.
The shelving on the wall were most likely those built by Georg Zweig.
Exterior of the building is below.
Barranquilla, Colombia
1940

Georg with the family pet, Fips.
Barranquilla, Colombia
1940

Erna and Georg
Barranquilla, Colombia
About 1947

Arnold
Barranquilla, Colombia
1952

Gerhard, left, with Arnold and their parents
Barranquilla, Colombia
1946

Arnold
Barranquilla, Colombia
1944

Arnold with two good friends;
Erich Reiss (L) and Mario Lustgarten (R)
Barranquilla, Colombia

Top, from left,
Inge Zweig (Peritz), Gerhard, Arnold, Gertrud Korach
Bottom, from left, Erna, Betty Zweig, Georg
Barranquilla, Colombia

House in the "El Prado" neighborhood of Barranquilla
Arnold lived here from 1946-1952.
In the foreground is his first car, a 1948 Pontiac
1944

Death certificate issued from Theresienstadt for Minna Korach.
*Photo courtesy of the National Archives, Prague*
*Terezín Initiative Institute*

their journey

# Uschi

I was an only child and my early childhood days were joyful and full of love. My parents, Arno and Hildegard Lehmann, were both born in Berlin, and stayed there as adults. I joined them on November 14, 1930.

I was given the name Ursula, which means "Little Bear", but I was called Uschi for as long as I can remember.

We had an apartment in the Neukölln area in the southeast area of Berlin, above the cleaning, pressing, and alterations store my parents owned and operated. Almost all of my uncles, aunts, and cousins were living in Berlin, as well as my Grandma and her youngest son, my Uncle Berthold. My grandmother and some of my cousins had cleaning stores similar to the one my parents owned. As a youngster, I was constantly surrounded by family who babysat me when I was very little or looked after me when the store became overly busy.

Our household was not a very religious one and we didn't keep kosher nor light the Sabbath candles on a regular basis although we did celebrate the major Jewish holidays. My Grandmother, on the other hand, did light the Sabbath candles and always made a traditional challah to celebrate when we visited on Friday evenings, which was often.

Naturally, I don't recall any of the political happenings in Germany at that time as I was much too young, but in retrospect I do recall that some of my relatives were leaving Berlin for the South American country of Colombia because the anti-Jewish sentiment in and around Berlin was getting unbearably worse. Unfortunately, it wasn't long before I experienced the reasons for their angst and understood for myself why they chose to leave Berlin.

When I was six years old my parents enrolled me in public school. It was a German custom for first time students to receive a *Schultüte*, a large cone filled with candy and sweets, to calm their nerves on the first day of school. A commemorative photo is also taken with the student holding a much larger cone, sometimes larger than the student themselves. The smiles and fun of school only lasted one year for me as *Kristallnacht*, the Night of Broken Glass, had occurred and increasing antisemitism had resulted in me being disallowed to attend public school and having to enroll in a Jewish school instead.

Kristallnacht happened during the night of November 9 and into the early morning hours of November 10, 1938, only two weeks before my eighth birthday. Prior to this horrific night the Nazis were largely non-violent towards the Jews and only instituted very oppressive rules and regulations. The Nazi policies were most likely made to encourage the Jewish people to leave, and leave they did. Large numbers of émigrés had already been fleeing the city thinking that life will undoubtedly become unlivable if they stayed in Berlin. The compass of humanity changed on that night that was Kristallnacht.

The community we lived in was not thought of as a Jewish community but a mix of both Jewish and Gentile businesses and apartments. Upon awakening the morning of November 10, we didn't even know what had happened throughout all the surrounding Jewish communities of Berlin. It was a regular work day for us, a Thursday. My father was in the bathroom shaving.

The phone rang.

A strange voice on the other end, an unknown male voice, said, "Get out of there or we're going to kill you."

My mother immediately called her mother, my Grandmother Gertrude. It turns out that her cleaning store which was in a Jewish neighborhood was ransacked and looted the previous night. My grandma told my parents to gather our essentials and to come stay at her apartment on Andrea Straße with her and Berthold until things settled down. My parents had always thought there was a Nazi living in our building and it's quite possible that he was the one who anonymously called to terrorize us but we'll never know. What I do know is that my parents and I left our shop and apartment that morning, leaving behind all of our equipment and our furniture, never to be seen again.

My grandmother had five children: my mother Hildegard, her youngest son Berthold who still lived with her, two other sons named Walter and Arnold, and a daughter named Käthe. Walter, Arnold, and Käthe had already emigrated from Berlin to Colombia about a year earlier, in 1937.

My parents and I were also supposed to go to Colombia a year earlier but my father was hesitant and even said "It can't be that bad. It's going to get better. The store is doing well. We'll wait a little to see what happens."

This sentiment was all too common in the community and eventually led to the slaughter of many people.

Even though my father was hesitant to leave Berlin, he did hire a Spanish teacher to come to the apartment twice a week to prepare us for a move, but we simply waited too long. Visas to get into Colombia and to be with the rest of our relatives were quickly running out and it was difficult to find any other country that was issuing entrance visas.

After moving in with my grandmother, we tried to get some semblance of normalcy back into our lives. Going back to school was a big part of it for me. I was enrolled into a girl's Jewish school in 1938 but that was short lived as the school was suddenly closed and converted into an infirmary for the German soldiers. I started going to another school for Jewish kids and it was here that I had my first experiences with anti-Semitic violence directed towards myself.

My classmates and I carried small square leather bound backpacks that we kept our books and school supplies in. I remember leaving school and seeing a group of Gentile boys waiting for us outside. They would grab us by the backpacks and throw us to the ground calling us names and hurling insults. This happened almost every day and it would always result in me running home in tears.

The Nazi antisemitism progressed rapidly and it became intolerable to continue going to school anymore, even a Jewish school. By late 1939 Hitler invaded Poland and World War II began. Jews were beginning to be systematically placed in Ghettos or were rounded up for concentration camps. We tried everything to not draw attention to ourselves to avoid being targeted. Jews in our community were mistreated with insults and there were signs everywhere saying we were not welcome. Imagine strolling the streets of your hometown, the place you grew up in, and seeing signs like *Juden werden hier nicht bedient*, Jews are not served here, or *Juden sind hier nicht erwunscht*, Jews are not welcome here. We were made to walk in the gutters, avoiding the cleaner sidewalks where the Gentile people were allowed. How did they know who was who? The Jews were forced to wear a badge, a small, Yellow Star of David made of cloth. We had to wear the star on our chest and there were heavy penalties if one was caught not wearing it. It was a horrible way for an eight year old to live, or anyone for that matter.

My Uncle Berthold eventually found a way to be smuggled out of Germany and into Belgium in May of 1942. I don't know the details of how he did it but it would be safe to assume that a fairly large sum of money was involved and an equal amount of danger. The Nazis were still encouraging the Jews to leave the country but with the limitations other countries were placing on refugees, it was nearly impossible for us to leave. Instead of just banishing Jews to ghettos, the Nazis began the systematic liquidation of thousands and thousands of people.

When I was born, there were about half a million Jews in Germany accounting for less than one percent of the general population, one third of them in Berlin alone. When Hitler came to power there was a surge of emigration to other European countries but a good number of Jews were later caught up in the Nazi progression to Western Europe and murdered. Many others left Europe altogether and went to exotic places like Shanghai, China or South America. Later research has shown that out of approximately 309,000 Jews within Europe only 27,000 had applied for United States visas.

By 1941 emigration for Jews out of Germany was strictly forbidden and many of the remaining 163,000 Jews that were left in the country were murdered in the Nazi death camps.

My Grandmother, Mother, Father, and I were eventually able to escape but it took quite a bit of effort amid the Nazi terror.

CR&O

The building we lived in with my Grandmother was a typical multi-story apartment building. We had enough space but little food. The Nazis had begun issuing everyone in Berlin ration coupons but the Jews were given special coupons entitling us to even less. It was not a pleasant existence for a little girl like me but we were strong and did what was necessary to survive, never giving up hope that we could get out of the country when the opportunity arose.

Our building had a cellar which the gentiles used for shelter during the constant aerial bombardments on Berlin. Since we were Jewish, we were forbidden from seeking safety in the cellar and instead had to weather the loud and incessant bombing from our apartment. Some of the bombs would fall silent right before they exploded and we were always terrified when heard such a device nearby, wondering if it would hit our building. To this day, I am still terrified of hearing things like fireworks and the like.

We received word from Berthold that he arrived in

the Belgian city of Brussels and that we should attempt to find a way to escape Berlin and find our way to his apartment. It was already 1942 and difficult to do anything. We were very limited to where we could go and the hours we could even be outside. Being outside the apartment at the wrong time would at best result in being beat up and at worst, being shot on the sidewalk. We began receiving word that our loved ones were being taken by the Nazis, first a cousin, then an aunt, then our neighbors. We knew they were taken away but had no idea where to or what had happened to them. Only that they were gone. You couldn't imagine the fear of going out as a Jew into such an environment. Occasionally the Nazis would bang on our front door, first demanding we give them all of our radios, then all of our jewelry. They ended up taking pretty much everything of value, including the lives of many family members.

One day towards the end of 1942 I remember hearing a commotion in our apartment. There was animated talking and discussions among the adults, phone calls, and people coming and going from the apartment. My parents received word that there were smugglers taking people to Belgium. We thought Belgium would be nicer and knew that my uncle was safely there so my parents made the arrangements for us to flee. For a Jewish person, to flee in late 1942 was not very common as those remaining in Germany were either in the camps or ghettos, had no means to pay a smuggler to flee, or were already murdered. We took advantage of the opportunity knowing full well the risks if we were caught.

My father had a fake passport and he left a few weeks before us to avoid any sort of suspicion. There were enough Nazi sympathizers in our neighborhood that had they seen us all leave together we would undoubtedly have been reported to the authorities.

The Nazis had youth groups and organizations, such as the Hitler Youth. There was another group composed of young girls, the *Bund Deutsche Mädel*, or BDM, and these girls had various outfits including a relatively colorful sweater. The smugglers were able to get a sweater for me to wear so I could disguise myself as a non-Jew. As we fled, I carried a baby doll with me, clutching her to my chest where the Yellow Star should have been, to avoid a snitch from saying they saw a Jew outside without their star.

It was nighttime when we fled and we were only allowed one suitcase. My mother packed clothes and some jewelry that she had been able to hide from the Nazis during their earlier rampage into the suitcase and off we went; myself, my mother, and my grandmother. I was a few weeks shy of my twelfth birthday.

The smugglers hurried us to a safe house and we waited. A few others also came to the house and we were quickly hustled to a waiting train which left after a very short wait. It was pitch black outside and I had absolutely no idea where the train was going. The silence within the train added to the tense and scary situation while strangely, the noise of the cold iron train tracks making their unmistakable clickity-clacking sounds was comforting.

The train stopped and we quickly exited and began to cross some sort of farm or pasture. The night sky around us was so dark we couldn't see where we were headed, so we focused on some dim lights at the far end of the land. I could hear cows with musical cowbells and I could sense their closeness to us but I couldn't see them in the darkness of the night. Someone, or a group of people, must have heard us crossing the field for suddenly with no warning there were gunshots ringing out. They were shooting at us. We immediately dropped to the manure sodden ground to avoid being shot. I could only imagine that it was just as difficult for the shooters to see us as it was for us to see them, thanks to the black night covering us and keeping us safe for the moment.

I have no idea how long we laid there but eventually a man, maybe a teenager, came by on a bicycle and helped me. My mother let me go with him, knowing that it would be impossible for me to make it on my own. The man took me to the lights we had seen on the far side of field which turned out to be a farmhouse. Shortly after, my grandmother and mother arrived there safely as well.

We stayed a short time at the farmhouse. While there, we were astonished to see that all the items in our luggage had been replaced with bricks. Even our smugglers, the ones helping us, resorted to stealing, leaving us with only the clothes on our backs. Soon we were escorted towards another train which we boarded. Finally, we were bound for Brussels.

When we arrived at the address that Uncle Berthold had provided for his apartment in Brussels, we were promptly told by the house lady that my Uncle was gone, the Nazis had taken him away. We had gone from one fire pit to another as the Nazis were systematically deporting and murdering Jews that were now living in Belgium. As it turned out, many Jews that had escaped Germany looking for a place to remain safe found themselves in another European country only to be caught up in more mass deportations and eliminations.

Finding a house where we could hide really didn't take too long. Belgium had a strong and extensive Resistance that formed after Hitler's army had invaded the country and an equal number of Belgians that were sympathetic to the Jewish refugees and took the incredible risk of hiding them.

Years after the Holocaust ended the State of Israel found a way to honor those non-Jews that risked their lives to help protect and save Jewish lives. Since 1963 an Israeli committee has taken the undertaking of documenting, evaluating, and then bestowing the "Righteous among the Nations" honor. Honorees are awarded a medal and their names are placed in the "Garden of the Righteous Among The Nations" in the Yad Vashem Holocaust Museum on the Mount of Remembrance in Jerusalem. Some well-known names such as Oskar Schindler, who saved the lives of twelve hundred Jews by employing them in his factories, are honored in this beautiful garden. Other lesser known individuals and families who risked their lives hiding one or two people are honored there as well, while others may have helped refugees but their acts of kindness and bravery were never known or acknowledged.

The family that hid me was never acknowledged…until now.

My mother and I had reconnected with my father and found a home on Chaussée de Haecht, not far from the center of Brussels, where a lady named Suzanne Saelens agreed to hide us. She was very nice to us, allowing us to stay in the small basement while she owned and ran a small Belgian pub which coincidentally catered to many German soldiers. She had arranged the basement to be as comfortable as possible but there really wasn't all too much that could be done to make it very homey. It was almost always dark as the basement windows were covered, mostly so that we would not be detected by others but also to block out light during the nightly aerial bombings. It was a drab existence but it was all I knew. I had some dolls to play with and occasionally a little girl that was younger than me would come downstairs to play with me. We never went outside except for on rare occasions to a small garden courtyard when it was safe to venture to without being seen by anyone.

CR80

My father found work in the same sort of cleaning business, much like we previously had in Berlin. We couldn't know it at the time, but we were about to feel our greatest loss.

One day in October, 1943, he went to his job via street car or tram. Most likely it was a cool autumn day, maybe a little rainy, and I'm sure he was wearing his favorite overcoat. He never returned home that night. Actually, he never returned home ever again.

When my father went to work that fateful day, he was renounced by a fellow Jew, a Polish Jew. It turns out that this man had lost his wife to the Gestapo and he had wanted to get even in some sort of sick way. He was a snitch hired by the Nazis to root out other Jews.

Most of the Jews captured in Brussels had been taken to a *Sammellager*, or transit camp, called Mechelen and placed in the old Dossin Barracks. The transit camp was between Antwerp and Brussels and near a major train line making this location a prime spot for deportations. More than twenty-five thousand Jews were rounded up and placed in this camp and held until further transit to the Auschwitz Concentration camp where they were enslaved, dehumanized, and eventually for many, gassed. Only about thirteen hundred were still alive when Auschwitz was liberated.

The prisoners in Mechelen were held until the camp reached a capacity of one thousand whereupon a train with Roman numeral designations would transport them to Auschwitz. In the time that Mechelen was open there were twenty eight such trains. The more infamous of these trains was Transit XX. This train had left Mechelen with 1,404 Jews and Romas (Gypsies) on board on April 19, 1943. Three Resistance members stopped the train and overtook the German guards. Over two hundred prisoners were able to escape although close to half of them were later captured. Over the years various documentaries have been produced about this very heroic action.

My father was taken to Mechelen, registered on October 9, 1943 and listed as prisoner number 263 on the deportation list for Transport XXIII. This Transport is known to have held 346 Jewish men and boys. It left Mechelen on January 14, 1944 and arrived at Auschwitz-Birkenau on January 17, three days later.

We received a handwritten note from him at the end of January 1944. The note was addressed to an acquaintance at an address other than where we were and it was brought over to us. Translated from German, it read:

*My dear.*
*I have arrived safely and healthy.*
*I am well.*
*Hope that you are healthy.*
*The morale is good.*
*Many heartfelt greetings from*
*Arno Lehmann*

The return address was from House 32 in
Monowitz, a sub-camp of the notorious Auschwitz
Concentration camp.

Monowitz, also known as Auschwitz III, was a
slave labor camp, an *Arbeitslager*. There were
many such camps in which large German
manufacturing firms would use the Jewish prisoners
as slave laborers. Conditions were deplorable and
those workers that could not produce any longer
were shipped to the gas chambers in Birkenau.

The letter that he wrote was most likely monitored
and probably was a form letter that many other
prisoners were forced to write, but at least it was
some sort of communication from him.
Unfortunately it was also the very last time we'd
hear from him.

Auschwitz was synonymous with death. It was
humankind at its worst depths and became a place
that many described as being nothing short of what

Hell must feel like. The number of people murdered at Auschwitz is largely unknown and may never be known with certainty. Some figures state that as many as two million Jews were tortured and murdered at this place at the hands of the Nazis. Torture and medical experimentation was common; families with children were stripped naked in the frigid European cold and marched to the gas chambers undoubtedly reciting Jewish prayers amongst themselves as they took their last gasps.

Nobel Prize winner, author, and Holocaust survivor Elie Wiesel wrote in his 1968 novel, *Legends of our Time*:

> **"At Auschwitz, not only man died, but also the idea of man. To live in a world where there is nothing anymore, where the executioner acts as God, as judge – many wanted no part of it. It was its own heart the world incinerated at Auschwitz"**

The solitary train track that took my father to those gates of Hell, behind which large smokestacks spewed the smoke and dust of hundreds of thousands of people, must have been a terrifying sight. Behind the gates my father probably saw many people wearing clothes resembling pajamas with bold vertical black stripes. I imagine his horror when he realized these were all prisoners and he was taken to a Concentration Camp, a death camp. As the trains pulled up, the occupants tugged and pulled on their large suitcases and carried them off the train as if they were merely relocating their living spaces for this camp. The SS guards yelled *Alle heraus, schneller!!*, Everyone out...faster! As the transport occupants disembarked, the guards took all their belongings and threw them into a huge pile, never to be seen by their owners again.

My father and all the other prisoners in Transport XXIII lined up. The SS at the head of the line sat there and played his little deadly game of cop, judge, jury, executioner, and God by determining who would live and who would die with a simple wave of his hand. You go to the right and you survive another day. You go to the left and you immediately get sent to the gas chambers. Families would do anything while in line to not only stay together, but to survive. Many heroic stories have been reported from people in line changing clothes with their parents so that their parents would look younger and thus spared the gas chamber. One story is of a mother and daughter who became separated from each other. The mother went to the left and the daughter went to the right. The daughter escaped from the holding area somehow, rescued her mother, and they got in line *again* and tried to elicit a different decision for her mother. They changed some clothes while in line and it worked. The brave, young daughter saved her mother's life.

Arno Lehmann was in good physical shape and he was sent to the right, tattooed with the number 172356 on his left forearm, and most likely sent to forced labor. Of the 346 men and boys on the Transport, only 140 survived that initial selection and were given tattooed numbers that ranged from 172296 to 172435. There is no information as to the site or type of forced labor he endured but it was most likely associated with the large chemical plant on the site.

The *Interessen-Gemeinschaft Farbenindustrie Werk Auschwitz,* or IG Farben, was a huge German conglomerate involved in chemicals and pharmaceuticals going back to the 1920's. Eventually, this company became heavily involved with the Nazi war effort and ended up enslaving about 80,000 Auschwitz prisoners for the purpose of fabricating synthetic rubber. It's very likely that this is where my father was initially assigned to work.

According to the records and documents found in Auschwitz, on March 28, 1944 my father was brought to the KL Auschwitz III-Monowitz hospital and spent the next twenty four days there. On April 21, 1944 he was taken away from the hospital and sent away to the KL Auschwitz II-Birkenau facility where he was most likely gassed to death. Arno Lehmann was just one of approximately one million people that records show were exterminated in just this one facility.

When my Uncle Berthold was captured on September 24, 1942 he had also been taken to the Dossin Barracks in Mechelen and registered as prisoner #2098. He was placed on Transport XI on September 26 and arrived at Auschwitz two days later.

For Berthold, there was no tattoo on his left forearm, there was no time to suffer in a labor camp or become a medical experiment in some crazed Nazi hands, and there was no death certificate for as he was waved to the left and immediately made the march to the gas chambers.

Hildegard Lehmann holding Uschi
Berlin, Germany
About May 1931

Arno and Hildegard Lehmann on
their wedding day. Hildegard was
21 and Arno was 22 years of age
Berlin, Germany
February 27, 1930

Uschi at 18 months of age.
Bad Salzelmen, Germany
May 15, 1932

Two typical storefronts in the early 1930's Berlin
To the left, Hildegard Lehmann stands in the doorway of the
family dry cleaning business. It's unknown if this is the one
destroyed during Kristallnacht. To the right is a bakery/pastry shop.
May 15, 1932

Uschi (arrow) accompanied this class of older students from the
Bergmanstraβe school on a field trip.
Berlin, Germany
1935

Uschi
Berlin, Germany
March 1934

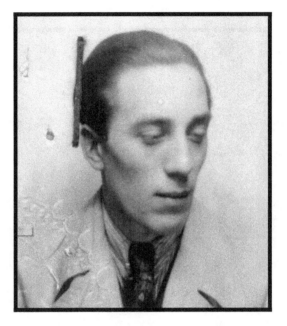

Berthold Schiemann
This is the last known photo of Berthold. The dark line to
the left is the staple which held this photo to a passport,
most likely a fake passport which he had with him when
he was taken in Brussels, Belgium.
About 1942
*Photo is courtesy of the Directorate-General War Victims
Brussels, Belgium*

This is a copy of the prisoner manifest for Transport XI which left Mechelen, Belgium on September 26, 1942 bound for Auschwitz. It shows Berthold Schiemann as prisoner #2098
*Transportlist Mechelen-Auschwitz, Transport XI, Page 107 – with the name Berthold Schiemann (Date of Birth Dec 21, 1918), held by the Archives Service for War Victims (State Archives of Belgium)*

Arno Anis Lehmann
This is the last known photo of Arno. Most likely the
photo was attached to the passport that was in his
possession when he was taken.
Brussels, Belgium.
About 1942
*Photo courtesy of the State Archives Belgium*
*Digitized by Kazerne-Dossin*

This is a copy of the *Registre Des Juifs*, the Jewish Registry, which was required of all Jews entering Belgium.
It shows Arno Lehmann entering Belgium on September 3, 1942, approximately one month prior to Uschi and Hildegard.
*Photo courtesy of the State Archives Belgium*
*Digitized by Kazerne-Dossin*

Copy of the prisoner manifest for Transport XXIII which left
Mechelen, Belgium on January 14, 1944 bound for Auschwitz.
It shows Arno Lehmann as prisoner #263. He was 36 years old.
*Transportlist Mechelen-Auschwitz, Transport XIII, Page 17 – with
the name Arno Lehmann (Date of Birth Nov 13, 1907), held by the
Archives Service for War Victims (State Archives of Belgium)*

One day Mrs. Saelens received a visit from a friend of hers. When her friend saw me in the basement she said, "I'll take you to where I live, out in the country, to Bourg-Léopold. I'll give you a new name and I'll take care of you."

My mother didn't want us to be separated, but she knew it would be safer for me so she approved and I went with this lady. She took me to the country in the Flemish part of Belgium and gave me the name of Jeanine Westerlain. I was enrolled in a school at the local convent for about six months, learned French and some Flemish very quickly, and became a pretty good student. I even picked up on the Christian catechisms that were taught, and was apparently one of the better students in the class.

The war continued to spread its ugly tentacles and it wasn't long before the convent was destroyed from aerial bombardments and another school experience ended for me.

Mother didn't want to be apart from me any longer so I went back to Brussels. Soon after I returned another round of air raid sirens went off. A bomb fell on the house directly behind us and exploded with a deafening noise. We had been standing outside by a wall and shrapnel hit me on my left side on my shoulder and very close to my temple. Suzanne was hit in the leg and I watched in horror as her whole leg was torn up.

This type of existence went on but we were still able to survive this terrible war. My grandmother's health was getting progressively worse and most of our days were spent in the basement or in the small garden taking care of her. Finally, in 1944 our city was liberated by the Americans. The beginning of the liberation occurred on D-Day in France and many felt that the German occupation would soon be done with. There was a man living upstairs from us who had a radio. He would listen to reports of the approaching American army and place pins in a map on the wall to indicate their advances. By this time, we started to feel a little safer leaving the basement and would listen to the radio as well to get any information we could about the outside world. When the city was finally liberated we went atop the balcony and saw the American and British troops driving along the streets. The horrible War was over!! I was not quite fourteen years old.

We moved out of the basement and my mother found a nice apartment for the three of us to live in. Grandmother was not getting better and was in and out of the hospital. I was finally able to attend school again. My new school was taught in French and because it was still a new language for me I had to enroll in one class lower than the one I should have been in, even though I did become fluent very quickly. I did well in school and eventually entered a professional school where I learned sewing, pattern making, fashion design, and secretarial skills. I also spent a lot of time care for my ailing grandmother as my own mother got a job at the local kosher butcher store.

We reconnected with my aunt and two uncles that emigrated to Colombia some years earlier and they invited us to meet them in Colombia. At the time, Grandmother was still very ill and it would have been impossible to make such a trip. After Grandmother died in March of 1948 my mother and I made arrangements for Colombia.

ॐ

We finally made our way to Colombia in January of 1949. My Aunt Käthe was living in Cali and her brothers were in Bogotá. The boat trip took three weeks but we didn't care as we were finally free from the European torment that consumed almost all of my first eighteen years.

We arrived at the port city of Barranquilla and one of my uncles met us there and brought us to his home in Bogotá. We stayed there for a few short

months and then went to Cali to stay with my aunt.
The stress of the previous few years finally caught
up with my mother and she suffered a nervous
breakdown. Thankfully, she recovered we decided
to move back to Bogotá and stay with my uncle
once again in his apartment.

I was fortunate to pick up the Spanish language as
rapidly as I did French. Doing so meant that I could
get a job and I began work in an engineering office
where I did quite well. Next, I worked in an
advertising agency and continued to excel in my
work and was eventually promoted to a manager
position. All this enabled my mother and I to get
our own apartment. I felt very proud!

My last job in Bogotá was in a factory that made
buttons and medals for the President. It was run by
a German fellow and his Spanish was poor so he
enlisted me to translate for him. I ended up having
my own secretary there and was doing nicely.

I would often vacation in Cali to visit my Aunt
Käthe. She had been friends back in Germany with
a family named Zweig. On Christmas Eve in 1954,
I accompanied her to visit them. Käthe told me that
the Zweig's had a very nice son who was a little
older than me, and he would be there as well.

Arnold Zweig and I met that late December day and
we have been together ever since. Our first day

together was spent visiting and talking. He had a record collection he was very proud of and was eager to play some music for me. We spent every day together for the next week. Arnold was very nice, very handsome, had a good job, and his parents were nice to me. We had only known each other a week but on New Year's Eve he proposed to me and I accepted. We immediately sent a cable to my mother back in Bogotá and she arrived in Cali for our engagement party. I spent a couple more weeks in Bogotá before having to return to my job in Cali. During our time apart, Arnold sent me many letters and flowers and he visited me as often as he could. We were married a few months later on May 9, 1955.

One would think that getting married after dating for only a week is a little crazy but consider this: we were two people that got caught up in a bad time in world history. For the most part, there was nothing that either one of us could have done to save our family members that perished. Instead, we went on with our lives and tried to survive as best we could. It was at times difficult but we did it. Being able to finally talk to someone that was not related to me and share similar stories was purely a divine intervention, a *Beshert*. A meeting of two people that a person named Hitler could not snuff out regardless of how hard he tried. A meeting that he had one day hoped would never happen again but he was wrong.

their journey

# Arnold & Uschi

Arnold and Uschi's wedding was not an overly lavish affair but it was a beautiful Jewish wedding. Their families were there, what was left of them, to celebrate with them. It was simple and they wore their nicest clothes; Arnold wore a perfect black suit with a tallis draped over his shoulder and Uschi wore a beautiful white wedding dress.

It was a bittersweet moment for everyone. For one, they remembered all those that couldn't be there to share in their joy. Uschi's father was of course not there and that was a sad thing. Her Uncle Arnold instead stood in his place. As Jews, they were glad that their lives would go on and the Jewish people as a whole could survive in the aftermath of the horrors everyone endured. By now, the war had been over for ten years and all the concentration camps were liberated. The world was still grasping the entirety of what had happened and the ensuing years brought forth many tales of heroism and weddings like theirs as well as countless tales of marriages destroyed by the Holocaust.

The genocide that the Jews of Europe suffered was enormous. Don't let anyone fool you into believing otherwise. It is estimated that up to two thirds of the European Jewry were murdered with almost ninety percent of Polish Jews murdered. It left countless families destroyed and created lasting scars that will never be healed. Hitler wanted to exterminate the Jews but he failed. A wedding uniting two survivors was the symbolic slap in the face to Hitler and European antisemitism. He was thankfully defeated but Arnold and Uschi were not. That was a victory.

Immediately after the wedding, Arnold and Uschi embarked on month long honeymoon. They stayed in Colombia and drove around the whole country exploring as much as they could. Back then Colombia was nothing like Europe was and to them it was quite primitive. The tropical weather in the lowlands was oppressive to say the least but they adapted very quickly and learned to like it.

The first night of their honeymoon they experienced a funny, yet embarrassing event, one they could laugh about for years…the bed broke! Rest assured, the details of the breakage will not be detailed here but the rest of their journey was breakage free.

Colombia in the mid 1950's was a very sleepy country. It was simple with plantations of coffee, stifling hot and humid coastal plains, and cool mountain cities. The people were all very nice and the newlywed's Spanish speaking skills were excellent. They remained fluent their whole lives and enjoyed conversing in the language to people in some of the many countries they later had the opportunity to visit.

When they arrived back in Cali after the honeymoon it was time to decide a few things, namely where they were going to live. Considering what they went through, having a safe place to live that was tolerant of religions was an important point. Uschi and her mother had decided a few years ago that they wanted to settle in the United States and their paperwork was completed some time ago. Arnold had visited the United States a few times previously during his importing/exporting work and found the USA to be a place where he would fit in and prosper.

Hildegard, Uschi's mother, had a friend in the city of Los Angeles and she encouraged her to emigrate there as well. Only a week or so after Uschi returned from her honeymoon, her mother did just that and moved to California. It was hardly a surprise that she was leaving as it was already discussed months ago but nonetheless it was sad to see her leave.

They decided not to go with her at the time as Uschi was pregnant with their first child. They thought it was best to delay their move until their child was born, mostly to avoid any sort of pregnancy complications during the hot and humid Colombian summer. This also gave them sufficient time to get everything in order with Arnold's work in Colombia.

Their daughter, Evelyn, was born on October 21, 1956. The delivery went quite well although Arnold paced so much outside the hospital that it's entirely possible he went through a complete pair of shoe soles. Their family helped them out quite a bit in learning the tips and tricks that new parents need to know and they were quite comfortable at being parents.

Of all their combined relatives who arrived in Colombia between 1935 and 1945, only one had decided to stay in the country and make it a permanent home. That was Uschi's Uncle Arnold. Everyone else decided to immigrate into other countries to find more suitable and appropriate long term situations.

Arnold's brother, Gerhard, met a young lady by the

name of Inge Peritz, who was a German survivor herself, and they left for New York when their daughter, Betty, was two years old. They arrived via the Cape Avinof liner in the Port of NY on April 6, 1951 and only eleven months later, on March 23, 1952, Gerhard passed away from a congenital heart ailment. It was quite sudden and Arnold and his mother hurried to New York as quickly as possible for his funeral.

After Evelyn's arrival, they finally were ready to make the move to the United States.

ᘒᘗᘖ

*"Give me your tired, your poor,*
*Your huddled masses yearning to breathe free,*
*The wretched refuse of your teeming shore.*
*Send these, the homeless, tempest-tossed to me,*
*I lift my lamp beside the golden door!"*

Many have probably read this portion of *New Colossus*, the beautiful sonnet written by Emma Lazarus that is inscribed on a bronze plaque adjacent to the Statue of Liberty. This last paragraph of that famous poem, written so many years before their arrival, was true for so many millions of people looking for a better life, for a better future, and for a country that didn't have the problems that they escaped in Europe. Their time in Colombia was good and they were extremely thankful to the Colombians for receiving them with open arms but it was time to move on. They had started a family and were anxious to establish some roots somewhere in this world.

In October 1957, the three of them boarded an American freighter, the SS Santa Flavia, and left Colombia for the shores of the United States. They arrived in the Port of Los Angeles (San Pedro) on October 21, 1957...Evelyn's first birthday.

Dwight D. Eisenhower was president, Elvis Presley was quickly gaining popularity, the California weather was much nicer than that of Colombia, and they were here to soak it all in. Like any immigrant, they wanted to assimilate as quickly as possible. Understanding the English language was really not that difficult as they had some previous English speaking experience although their thick accents were difficult to mask.

They only had the few belongings they brought with them as they were ready for a fresh start in this new country. Arnold quickly found work in the export and import business. Uschi's mother had an apartment in downtown Los Angeles that had plenty of room for the three of them and they ended up staying there for a short time. Eventually, they found an apartment not far from Uschi's mother and moved out to their very own place.

They were also busy with one more venture… Uschi was pregnant with their second child. Their son, David, was born in December 1958 and in homage to President Eisenhower, who was president when they set foot in the United States, they named him after the President's father.

Life in California was very good and they quickly desired the quintessential suburb existence that so many people in the world strive for. They were living in the city, close to downtown, but wanted a larger place for the growing family so they opted to find a place in the suburbs of Los Angeles. Arnold was doing well with his new work as an insurance salesman for a very large insurance company and was able to afford a small home.

Uschi had begun to go by her middle name, Lanny. It was easier for people to pronounce and she was very comfortable with it. Assimilating into the States can be challenging so why not start with a name that was easier to pronounce and spell than Uschi? In a short time, everyone was calling her Lanny except friends of her mother and other German immigrants that still knew her as Uschi.

Their family continued to grow and fill their

suburban home. They had a second daughter, Peggy, who was born in October of 1960 and then came another son, Milton, who arrived in December 1963. As they did with David, the name Milton was in honor of the United States President at the time of their immigration but this time choosing the name of one of Eisenhower's brothers.

Many American immigrants consider becoming a naturalized citizen and of course, Arnold and Lanny were no exception. For the most part, besides being welcomed in the United States, they felt pretty much stateless. They had not been back to Germany in many years and always felt that Colombia had been a stepping stone of sorts. Becoming U.S. citizens seemed a natural progression and they decided to go ahead with the proper sponsorship forms and red tape. Arnold was the first to achieve citizenship, doing so in 1972. Lanny waited longer and became a citizen in 2002.

CB8O

Arnold and Lanny's story is a common one. The names and faces are different from other stories yet the theme is all too common. The strife and conflict around the world will only create more opportunity for families to be torn apart, for people to flee their homes out of fear, for governments to create situations in which an ethnic group is targeted for murder and elimination.

We teach our children to Never Forget, but do they? Our schools attempt to teach equality and tolerance, but do they? Our politicians seem to listen to their constituents as they march or send letters asking to pass legislation to fight antisemitism, to overcome racism, or to help other refugees who are in the exact situation Arnold and Lanny were in when countries closed their borders to them, but do they?

The answers to these questions are not in their story but if it enables future generations, additional schools, and new politicians to gain a better understanding of what hate and war do to people then perhaps telling this story is not in vain.

The two of them have seen and experienced their unfair share of what the bad in people can do yet they have seen much more good in humanity. They have persevered! They survived and they thrived!

Rabbi Harold Kushner wrote a very popular book titled "*When Bad Things Happen to Good People*" which tried to deal with this eternal question.

He wrote,

**"Is there an answer to the question of why bad things happen to good people?...The response would be...to forgive the world for not being perfect, to forgive God for not making a better world, to reach out to the people around us, and to go on living despite it all...no longer asking why something happened, but asking how we will respond, what we intend to do now that it has happened."**

For all of their future generations, Arnold and Lanny couldn't have said it any better than that.

their journey

The Schiemann brothers and sisters that reunited in Colombia.
From left, Walter Schiemann, Hildegard, Käthe, and Arnold
Schiemann. Walter and Käthe both ended up moving back to Berlin.
They died in 1988 and 1993 respectively. Arnold remained in
Colombia for many years.

Hildegard (L) and Uschi
Colombia
Date unknown

Gertrude Berlowski
Uschi's Grandmother
Date and location unknown

Käthe Cohn (Schiemann) Cali,
Colombia
1952

Uschi
Bogotá, Colombia
About 1953

Uschi at her engagement party
Cali, Colombia
January, 1955

This is a poem, one of many, that Arnold wrote to Uschi after the engagement when she had to return to Bogotá and her job. It translates as:

*For Uschi,*
*The fulfillment of a dream...*
*A dream of fulfillment.*

*With the love that a man can have only for his wife, or for her who will become his wife.*
*Arnold*
*January 17, 1955*

Erna and Georg escort Arnold prior to the wedding,
Cali, Colombia
May 9, 1955

May 9, 1955

First post wedding kiss
May 9, 1955

Honeymoon
May, 1955

Honeymoon
May, 1955

Honeymoon
May, 1955

Arnold holding Evelyn
Colombia
Spring 1957

The author with Mom
Santa Monica, California
June, 1964

Peggy (Left), Milton, Evelyn
Van Nuys, California
Spring 1964

Clockwise from top left,
Milton, David, Evelyn, Peggy
Carlsbad, California
2017

Arnold and Lanny return to Germany and Belgium
for the first time since the end of the War
1971

New Year's Eve
Carlsbad, California
2008

Arnold and Lanny
Carlsbad, California
2016

*Epilogue*

In the fall of 2016 I had come across an old and incomplete typed manuscript that my father had written. I had never seen it and was astonished to see that it was the beginning of his life story. I have no doubt that his work in translating the memoirs of his great-Grandfather, Henry Cohn, played a huge part in providing the stimulus in writing his own memoirs.

The manuscript had dates crossed out on the top going back to the early 1980's and represented the revisions he had done. Unfortunately his written recollections ended about the time of his seventh or eighth birthday... there was much more to write and I had an idea. I approached my parents and attempted to find out if any more of the story had been written and where it might be. There was none.

Their memories by this time had become muted and I realized that there was a very short window to sit with both of them and hear more of their individual stories and of how they met. I had seen a 1995 recording of them which was done for the USC Shoah Foundation but at the time I was finishing dental school and hadn't fully realized its significance or the impact it would have on me.

I decided to write this book after hearing their stories.

It was amazing that they still knew many of the minute details of their life, of who they met over the years, and of the horrors they saw and I was able to piece together their stories through research and activities that were going on at the time. They had boxes of old photos, some dating back to the late 1800's and they even remembered the names of many of their cousins and friends that were taken in the Holocaust... and there were many.

In particular, I wanted to find out as much as possible about Arno Lehmann, my Grandfather. I contacted the Kazerne-Dossin Museum located in the Mechelen suburb of Brussels, Belgium and was able to access their database of those captured and find some very interesting data about Arno, including his last known address, when he was transported, the number he was assigned, his last known photo and his eventual fate. The emotions came pouring out when I realized that this photo was the last one ever taken of him.

Various organizations have been established over the years since the War ended for the purpose of helping families of survivors find out what happened to their loved ones. The amount of information continues to be published online and archived and is now accessible with only a few mouse clicks. Unfortunately, there is still quite a bit of archived information held in Russia that is inaccessible. It wasn't until 2017 that the Wiener Library in London was able to procure a treasure trove of information that had been collected by the UN war crimes commission dating back to 1943. The website of the Wiener Library is available to the public.

The International Tracing Service, ITS, based in Bad Arolsen, Germany, was established in 1943 by the British Red Cross to facilitate searches of those displaced, incarcerated, or murdered during WWII. The ITS website reads "This unique archive contains over 30 million pages of Holocaust-era documents relating to the fates of over 17.5 million people who were subject to incarceration, forced labour and displacement during and after World War II." This information is available online as well and there is a reading room within the Bad Arolsen facility.

This whole project was an emotional one yet needed to be done to memorialize not only their story but a

time period in which some people *still* think never
happened.  As of this writing, there are fewer than
100,000 Survivors still alive and the memories are
quickly disappearing.

Arnold and Lanny Zweig eventually purchased a
larger home for their family in the Studio City
suburb of Los Angeles in 1974.  Arnold retired in
1981 and in 2001 they moved to the La Costa Glen
retirement community in Carlsbad, California where
they still reside.

Besides enjoying frequent visits from children,
grandchildren, and great grandchildren they are still
very active with their friends and community
activities.

Erna and Georg Zweig left Colombia in the late
1950's and moved back to Berlin.  Georg died in
1962.  Erna moved back to the U.S. for a short time
in the 1970's and lived in an apartment close to
Arnold and the family but she never felt very
comfortable in the U.S.  She again moved back to
Berlin and died there in 1986.

Hildegard Lehman continued to live in the Fairfax
area of Los Angeles with a partner named Sam
Stern.  I never had a grandfather as a child and I
always assumed that Sam was my grandpa.  He
treated us very well and spoiled us.  I still remember
the summer days when my brother and I would

coax him into driving us in his white Mercury
Cougar just to get 7-11 Slurpees. He worked for the
studios doing prop construction and whenever we
watched television he would point out what he built.
I'm pretty sure he exaggerated but for a five or six
year old I was very impressed. I had the
opportunity to spend a month with my Oma
Hildegard in Berlin during the summer of 1980
when she visited her brother and sister that lived
there. It was here that the first signs of Alzheimer's
disease became evident and she passed away in
1996, in Studio City, CA, as a result of
complications of the disease.

My mother had a cousin that escaped Berlin via the
*Kindertransport* and eventually settled in London.
He had a daughter with whom I am in contact with.
I was able to find out the exact transport her father
and been on and was actually able to contact a
gentleman in London that *knew* him as they had
been on the very same transport! He was in his late
90's and could not provide me any other
information.

Finally, the internet now has so many features that
enable research into the past. In doing my research
and collecting and reviewing previous research
done by my father and others I have been able to
piece together a very comprehensive family tree
that goes back over 200 years and includes

hundreds of people.  As of now, an ever increasing family tree can be easily seen via the genealogical website, Ancestry.com.   It is titled "Zweig Family Tree".

CPSIA information can be obtained
at www.ICGtesting.com
Printed in the USA
LVHW091803150621
690286LV00007B/1214

9 781986 514415